Orange **Line 3**

Vokabellernheft Grundkurs

Ernst Klett Verlag
Stuttgart • Leipzig

Vorwort

Dieses Vokabellernheft im Taschenformat enthält alle Wörter und Wendungen aus *Orange Line* 3 Grundkurs. Aufgrund seines praktischen Formats kannst du es überall hin mitnehmen, um deine Wörter zu lernen und zu wiederholen.
Am besten hast du beim Lernen immer einen Bleistift zur Hand. Damit markierst du Wörter und Wendungen, die dir besondere Schwierigkeiten bereiten. Diese kannst du dann in regelmäßigen Abständen immer wieder durchgehen.
Am Ende jeder Unit findest du zahlreiche Übungen, mit denen du das Gelernte wiederholen, ordnen und dich auf Vokabeltests vorbereiten kannst.

Viel Spaß wünscht dir dein *Orange-Line*-Team!

Unit 1 What's your game?

Check-in

home [həʊm]	Heimat, Heimat-
rugby ['rʌgbi]	Rugby
century ['sentʃri]	Jahrhundert
its [ɪts]	sein/seine; ihr/ihre
American football [əˌmerɪkən 'fʊtbɔːl]	Football
player ['pleɪə]	Spieler/Spielerin, Mitspieler/Mitspielerin
helmet ['helmət]	Helm
during (+ noun) ['djʊərɪŋ]	während (+ Nomen)
each [iːtʃ]	jede/jeder/jedes
to **catch, caught, caught** [kætʃ, kɔːt, kɔːt]	fangen, erreichen
stadium ['steɪdiəm]	Stadion
you [juː; jə]	man
to **learn** [lɜːn]	erfahren
bat [bæt]	Schläger
glove [glʌv]	Handschuh
rugby boot [ˌrʌgbi 'buːt]	Rugbyschuh, Stollenschuh
fact box ['fækt bɒks]	Infokasten
baseball ['beɪsbɔːl]	Baseball
batter ['bætə]	Schlagmann/Schlagfrau
to **score** [skɔː]	punkten, ein Tor schießen
run [rʌn]	Runde
action ['ækʃn]	Handlung, Aktion
stand [stænd]	Tribüne
to **go with** ['gəʊ‿wɪð]	passen zu
against [ə'genst]	gegen
ambulance ['æmbjələns]	Krankenwagen
building ['bɪldɪŋ]	Gebäude

Language

they [ðeɪ]	hier: man
pitch [pɪtʃ]	Spielfeld

national ['næʃnl]	National-, landesweit
best [best]	am besten
beach [bi:tʃ]	Strand
court [kɔ:t]	Spielfeld
net [net]	Netz
across [ə'krɒs]	über, hinüber, quer durch/ darüber
sand [sænd]	Sand
goalkeeper ['gəʊlˌki:pə]	Torwart
back line [ˌbæk 'laɪn]	Grundlinie
to **kill** [kɪl]	töten; hier: tot machen
signal ['sɪgnl]	Zeichen
full (of) [fʊl]	ganz, voll (von/mit)
birth [bɜ:θ]	Geburt
height [haɪt]	Höhe, Größe
weight [weɪt]	Gewicht
foot, feet (pl) [fʊt; fi:t]	Fuß (Längenmaß: 30,48 cm)
inch [ɪnʃ]	Zoll (Längenmaß: 2,54cm)
gramme (g) [græm]	Gramm
union ['ju:njən]	Liga; Vereinigung, Union
was/were born [bɔ:n]	wurde(n) geboren
about [ə'baʊt]	ungefähr, circa, etwa

Everyday English

could [kʊd]	könnte/könnten
lad [læd]	Junge
half-price [ˌhɑ:f'praɪs]	zum halben Preis
What time ...? [wɒt 'taɪm]	(Um) wie viel Uhr ...?
Cor! [kɔ:]	Mann!
bloody ['blʌdi]	blutig; hier: verdammt
ref(eree) [ˌrefr'i:]	Schiedsrichter/Schieds-richterin
foul [faʊl]	Foul
fair [feə]	gerecht, fair
to **send off** [send‿'ɒf]	vom Platz verweisen
score [skɔ:]	Punktestand, Spielstand
It's a draw. [ˌɪts‿ə 'drɔ:]	Es steht unentschieden.
BC (= before Christ) [bi:'si:]	vor Christus

post [pəʊst] Pfosten, Mast
cup [kʌp] Pokal; Tasse, Kelch
world [wɜ:ld] Erde, Welt

Get fit!

catcher ['kætʃə] Fänger/Fängerin
base [beɪs] Base
pitcher ['pɪtʃə] Pitcher/Pitcherin
home plate ['həʊm ˌpleɪt] Home Plate
at the bottom [ət ðə 'bɒtəm] unten, im unteren Teil
at the top [ət ðə 'tɒp] oben, im oberen Teil
enough [ɪ'nʌf] genug, genügend
to **be missing** [bi: 'mɪsɪŋ] fehlen

Overheard

tennis ['tenɪs] Tennis
row [rəʊ] Reihe
British ['brɪtɪʃ] britisch

Facts and fiction

practice ['præktɪs] Training
nearly ['nɪəli] fast, annähernd
doorstep ['dɔ:step] Türstufe
next door [ˌnekst 'dɔ:] nebenan
to **moan** [məʊn] (sich) (be)klagen, stöhnen
to **dig up, dug up, dug up** [dɪg‿'ʌp, dʌg‿'ʌp, dʌg‿'ʌp] ausgraben
lonely ['ləʊnli] einsam
to **feel sorry for** [fi:l 'sɒri] Mitleid haben mit, bedauern
fight [faɪt] Kampf
thick [θɪk] dick (nicht für Personen); dumm
to **come down** [kʌm 'daʊn] herunterkommen, sich legen
to **substitute** ['sʌbstɪtju:t] auswechseln, ersetzen
What a laugh! [ˌwɒt‿ə 'lɑ:f] Wie lustig!
to **run into** [rʌn‿'ɪntə] laufen gegen, stoßen gegen
to **knock out** [nɒk‿'aʊt] k.o. schlagen, umhauen

himself [hɪm'self]	sich (selbst)
crowd [kraʊd]	Menschenmenge
rest [rest]	Rest

Words in action

the same [seɪm]	derselbe/dieselbe/dasselbe; gleich

1 Sports

Ergänze die fehlenden Buchstaben.

1. r__g__y	5. p__ tc__
2. pla__e__	6 g__alk__ep__r
3. ba__e__a__l	7. b__ ck __ine
4. st__d__u__	8. __c__c__ee

2 Nouns

Verbinde die Nomen richtig.

1. American	post
2. rugby	football
3. back	plate
4. fact	line
5. home	boot
6. goal	box

3 Odd one out

Welches Wort fällt aus der Reihe?

1. court	stadium	cup
2. catcher	doorstep	player
3. football	referee	baseball
4. century	inch	BC
5. stand	height	weight
6. birth	beach	sand

4 Baseball

Welche Wörter fallen dir zum Thema „Baseball" ein?

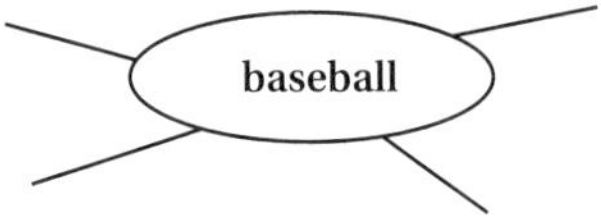

5 Little words

Wie heißen die kleinen Wörter?

1. ungefähr ______________ 4. fast, annähernd ______________

2. man ______________ 5. genug ______________

3. gegen ______________ 6. über, hinüber ______________

6 Opposites

Finde das Gegenteil.

1. at the top ______________

2. empty ______________

3. new ______________

7 Nouns from verbs

Bilde Nomen, indem du „-er" an die Verben anhängst.

1. to catch ______________ 4. to play ______________

2. to bat ______________ 5. to teach ______________

3. to sing ______________ 6. to report ______________

8 Words for pictures

Finde die richtigen Wörter zu den Bildern.

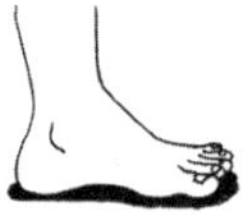

1. ______________________

2. ______________________

3. ______________________

4. ______________________

9 Plurals

Wie lautet die Mehrzahl?

1. cup ______________________
2. century ______________________
3. pitch ______________________
4. foot ______________________
5. referee ______________________
6. goalkeeper ______________________

10 Verbs

In dieser Unit hast du einige Verben zum Thema „Sport" gelernt. Kannst du dich an alle erinnern? Schreibe sie auf.

____

____

11 The letter 'o'

In diesen Wörtern kommt überall der Buchstabe „o" vor, aber er wird nicht immer gleich ausgesprochen. Sortiere die Wörter.

across score row born post lonely
knock home glove stone

[əʊ]	[ɒ]
______________________	______________________
______________________	______________________
[ɔː]	**[ʌ]**
______________________	______________________
______________________	______________________

12 Difficult words

Welche Wörter fallen dir noch schwer? Schreibe sie auf und wiederhole sie noch einmal.

____

____

Unit 2 Out and about in London

Check-in

capsule ['kæpsju:l]	Kapsel
spectacular [spek'tækjələ]	spektakulär
view [vju:]	Aussicht, Sicht
palace ['pælɪs]	Palast
royal ['rɔɪəl]	königlich
to **relive** [ˌri:'lɪv]	noch einmal erleben
great [greɪt]	groß
queue [kju:]	(Warte-)Schlange
traffic jam ['træfɪk ˌdʒæm]	Stau
traffic ['træfɪk]	Verkehr
Tube [tju:b]	Londoner U-Bahn
to **go far** [gəʊ 'f]ɑ:]	weit kommen, es weit bringen
trendy ['trendi]	modisch
king [kɪŋ]	König
to **build, built, built** [bɪld, bɪlt, bɪlt]	bauen
tower ['taʊə]	Turm
valuable ['væljuəbl]	wertvoll
jewel ['dʒu:əl]	Juwel
crown [kraʊn]	Krone
underground ['ʌndəgraʊnd]	U-Bahn
to **have breakfast** [hæv 'brekfəst]	frühstücken

Language

local ['ləʊkl]	lokal, örtlich
newspaper ['nju:sˌpeɪpə]	Zeitung
pickpocket ['pɪkˌpɒkɪt]	Taschendieb/Taschendiebin
tourist ['tʊərɪst]	Tourist/Touristin
to **change** [tʃeɪndʒ]	umsteigen
thanks to ['θæŋks tə]	dank (dir/ihnen), wegen
to **rob** [rɒb]	rauben, ausrauben
within [wɪ'ðɪn]	innerhalb

teenager ['tiːnˌeɪdʒə]	Teenager, Jugendliche/ Jugendlicher
busy ['bɪzi]	belebt
handbag ['hænbæg]	Handtasche
businessman ['bɪznɪsmən]	Geschäftsmann
rucksack ['rʌksæk]	Rucksack
finally ['faɪnli]	endlich
cathedral [kə'θiːdrl]	Kathedrale, Dom
toy [tɔɪ]	Spielzeug
fine [faɪn]	Geldbuße, Geldstrafe
rich [rɪtʃ]	reich
one(s) [wʌn(z)]	(Platzhalter für ein Nomen)
to **become, became, become** [bɪ'kʌm, bɪ'keɪm, bɪ'kʌm]	werden
blond(e)-haired ['blɒnd ˌheəd]	blond
actress ['æktrəs]	Schauspielerin
model ['mɒdl]	Model; Modell
sporty ['spɔːti]	sportlich
prince [prɪns]	Prinz
souvenir [ˌsuːvə'nɪə]	Souvenir, Andenken

Everyday English

coach [kəʊtʃ]	Reisebus
post office ['pəʊstˌɒfɪs]	Postamt
pier [pɪə]	Pier, Landungssteg
to **get to** ['get tə]	kommen zu, kommen nach, erreichen
corner ['kɔːnə]	Ecke
coffee ['kɒfiː]	Kaffee
side [saɪd]	Seite
population [ˌpɒpjə'leɪʃn]	Bevölkerung
fact file (on) [ˌfækt 'faɪl]	Ordner mit Informationen (über)
metre ['miːtə]	Meter
hotel suite [həʊ'tel ˌswiːt]	Hotelsuite
hotel [həʊ'tel]	Hotel
per [pɜː]	pro
kilometre ['kɪləʊˌmiːtə; kɪ'lɒmɪtə]	Kilometer

transport (no pl.) ['trænspɔ:t]	Verkehrsmittel, Beförderung
day travel card [ˌdeɪ 'trævl ˌkɑ:d]	Tagesfahrkarte

Get fit!

baker ['beɪkə]	Bäcker/Bäckerin
to **put out** [pʊt‿'aʊt]	ausmachen; löschen
fire [faɪə]	Feuerstelle; Kaminfeuer
to **smell, smelt, smelt** [smel, smelt, smelt]	riechen
smoke [sməʊk]	Rauch
flame [fleɪm]	Flamme
to **blow, blew, blown** [bləʊ, blu:, bləʊn]	wehen, blasen
to **burn, burnt, burnt** [bɜ:n, bɜ:nt, bɜ:nt]	(ver)brennen
fire brigade ['faɪə brɪˌgeɪd]	Feuerwehr
to **destroy** [dɪ'strɔɪ]	zerstören
boat [bəʊt]	Boot, Schiff

Overheard

to **get on** [get‿'ɒn]	einsteigen (in Zug, Bus ...)
dialogue ['daɪəlɒg]	Dialog, Gespräch

Facts and fiction

courier ['kʊriə]	Kurier
pollution [pə'lu:ʃn]	(Umwelt-)Verschmutzung
to **argue** ['ɑ:gju:]	streiten, argumentieren
to **carry** ['kæri]	befördern
tin [tɪn]	Dose, Büchse
milkman, milkmen (pl) ['mɪlkmən; 'mɪlkmen]	Milchmann
tradition [trə'dɪʃn]	Tradition
dairy ['deəri]	Molkerei
company ['kʌmpəni]	Gesellschaft, Firma; Kompanie

at the crack of dawn [ˌkræk‿əv ˈdɔːn]	im Morgengrauen
dawn [dɔːn]	Morgendämmerung, Tagesanbruch
to **deliver** [dɪˈlɪvə]	(aus)liefern
customer [ˈkʌstəmə]	Kunde/Kundin
since [sɪnts]	seit, seitdem
taxi [ˈtæksi]	Taxi
like the back of my hand [ˈbæk‿əv maɪ ˌhænd]	wie meine Westentasche
kind [kaɪnd]	Art, Sorte
especially [ɪˈspeʃli]	besonders
to **expect** [ɪkˈspekt]	erwarten
punk [pʌŋk]	Punk
style [staɪl]	Stil; hier: Frisur
regular [ˈregjələ]	Stammkunde/Stammkundin
to **get interested** [get ˈɪntrəstɪd]	sich interessieren
mess [mes]	Durcheinander, Unordnung

1 Adjectives

Setze die richtigen Adjektive ein.

scary trendy expensive spectacular rich

1. The views from the London Eye are ________________ .
2. The shops in London are very ________________ .
3. A lot of ________________ people live in London.
4. They can buy ________________ houses.
5. The London Dungeon is really ________________ .

2 Word puzzle

Finde die 15 Wörter im Puzzle. Sie sind senkrecht, waagerecht und diagonal versteckt.

after, busy, courier, finally, for, jewel, newspaper, queue, prince, regular, royal, since, taxi

R	F	D	J	J	S	N	O	N	R
M	O	A	R	E	W	E	C	T	E
F	R	Y	K	W	F	W	O	P	G
C	L	F	A	E	B	S	U	R	U
T	A	X	I	L	U	P	R	I	L
H	S	I	N	C	E	A	I	N	A
B	U	S	Y	L	U	P	E	C	R
I	A	G	A	F	T	E	R	E	K
F	S	K	E	E	T	R	F	G	N
A	D	C	H	F	J	E	N	T	D
S	D	L	C	Q	U	E	U	E	H
F	I	N	A	L	L	Y	E	R	L

3 Buildings

Welche Gebäude kennst du?

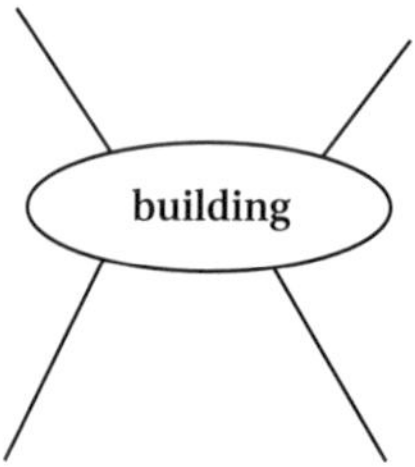

4 Odd one out

Welches Wort fällt aus der Reihe?

1. palace	crown	underground
2. tower	teenager	building
3. handbag	tin	rucksack
4. fire	flame	pier
5. milkman	kind	dairy

5 Verbs

Verbinde die Wörter richtig.

1. to go	interested
2. to come	out
3. to put	far
4. to get	true

6 In London

Ergänze die fehlenden Buchstaben.

1. b__il__i__g
2. de__i__er
3. __ol__u__i__n
4. mi__km__n
5. tr__di__i__n
6. j__w__l
7. bu__n
8. co__p__ny

7 Little words

Wie heißen die kleinen Wörter?

1. innerhalb ______________
2. nachdem ______________
3. Viertel ______________
4. endlich ______________
5. seit, seitdem ______________

8 Comparisons

Setze die richtigen Wörter ein.

oldest faster trendiest scariest best

1. The London Dungeon is the ____________________ museum in London.
2. You can get the ____________________ views of London from the London Eye.
3. The Tube is ____________________ than the bus.
4. Some of the ____________________ shops are in the King's Road.
5. The Tower is one of the ____________________ buildings in London.

9 Adjectives

Wie heißen diese Adjektive auf Englisch?

1. spektakulär ____________________
2. größer ____________________
3. der/die/das gruseligste ____________________
4. der/die/das modischste ____________________
5. wertvoller ____________________
6. belebt ____________________

10 Mixed up words

Welche Wörter sind hier durcheinander geraten?

1. weiv ______________________________
2. evlrie ______________________________
3. drneudonrug ______________________
4. kpocicpket _________________________

11 Who am I?

Finde die richtigen Buchstaben.

1. The first letter of 'prince'. ____
2. The fourth letter of 'population'. ____
3. The sixth letter of 'souvenir'. ____
4. The third letter of 'baker'. ____
5. I usually have colourful hair. ______________________

12 Hard or easy?

Diese Wörter fand ich in Unit 2 besonders ….

einfach	schwierig
________________________	________________________
________________________	________________________
________________________	________________________

Unit 3 Here we come!

Check-in

United Kingdom (UK) [juːˌnaɪtɪd 'kɪŋdəm]	Vereinigtes Königreich von Großbritannien und Nordirland
coastline ['kəʊstˌlaɪn]	Küstenlinie
to **travel** ['trævl]	reisen
cliff [klɪf]	Klippe
ancient ['eɪnʃnt]	alt, antik
circle ['sɜːkl]	Kreis
almost ['ɔːlməʊst]	fast, beinahe
officer ['ɒfɪsə]	Beamter/Beamtin
smuggler ['smʌglə]	Schmuggler/Schmugglerin
to **take** [teɪk]	dauern, (Zeit) brauchen
anywhere ['eniweə]	überall; irgendwo
channel ['tʃænl]	Kanal; Programm
ferry ['feri]	Fähre
to **land** [lænd]	landen
international [ˌɪntə'næʃnl]	international
passenger ['pæsndʒə]	Passagier/Passagierin, Beifahrer/Beifahrerin
port [pɔːt]	Hafen
cruise [kruːz]	Kreuzfahrt
ocean liner ['əʊʃn ˌlaɪnə]	Ozeandampfer
ocean ['əʊʃn]	Ozean
to **sail** [seɪl]	segeln, fahren (Schiff)
speaker ['spiːkə]	Sprecher/Sprecherin
swimmer ['swɪmə]	Schwimmer/Schwimmerin

Language

sun [sʌn]	Sonne
paradise ['pærəˌdaɪs]	Paradies
swimsuit ['swɪmsuːt]	Badeanzug
on record [ɒn 'rekɔːd]	verzeichnet, dokumentiert
clean [kliːn]	sauber
sandy ['sændi]	sandig

lifeguard ['laɪfgɑ:d]	Rettungsschwimmer/ Rettungsschwimmerin
swimming pool ['swɪmɪŋ ˌpu:l]	Schwimmbecken; Schwimmbad
sensible ['sensɪbl]	vernünftig
to **fly** [flaɪ]	wehen
safe [seɪf]	sicher
to **windsurf** ['wɪnsɜ:f]	windsurfen
to **canoe** [kə'nu:]	Kanu fahren
age [eɪdʒ]	Alter; Zeitalter
bin [bɪn]	Mülleimer, Mülltonne
to **be lost** [bi: 'lɒst]	sich verirrt haben
alone [ə'ləʊn]	allein
to **dive** [daɪv]	tauchen
stranger ['streɪndʒə]	Fremder/Fremde
rubber ring [ˌrʌbə 'rɪŋ]	Schwimmreifen
rubber ['rʌbə]	Gummi; Kautschuk
ring [rɪŋ]	Ring
wood [wʊd]	Holz
p.m. [ˌpi:'em]	nachmittags (Uhrzeit)
stamp [stæmp]	Briefmarke

Everyday English

lake [leɪk]	See
Cornish ['kɔ:nɪʃ]	kornisch; aus Cornwall
Welsh [welʃ]	walisisch; Waliser/Waliserin
distance ['dɪstns]	Distanz, Entfernung
quarter ['kwɔ:tə]	Viertel
stone [stəʊn]	brit. Gewichtseinheit (= 6,35kg)
yard [jɑ:d]	Elle (Längenmaß: 0,914 m)

Get fit!

to **be sorry** [bi: 'sɒri]	Leid tun
meat [mi:t]	Fleisch
passports (pl) ['pɑ:spɔ:ts]	Passkontrolle
passport ['pɑ:spɔ:t]	Pass, Reisepass

trolley ['trɒli]	Gepäckwagen, Einkaufswagen, Handkarren
phone box ['fəʊn ˌbɒks]	Telefonzelle

Facts and fiction

to **stand, stood, stood** [stænd, stʊd, stʊd]	stehen
to **notice** ['nəʊtɪs]	bemerken
to **trust** [trʌst]	vertrauen
whom [hu:m]	dem, der (Relativpronomen)
mother ['mʌðə]	Mutter
father ['fɑ:ðə]	Vater
tug [tʌg]	Ziehen, Zupfen
to **take off** [teɪk‿'ɒf]	ausziehen, abnehmen
to **rest** [rest]	sich ausruhen, sich entspannen
this evening [ðɪs 'i:vnɪŋ]	heute Abend
basement ['beɪsmənt]	Kellergeschoss, Untergeschoss
blind [blaɪnd]	blind
although [ɔ:l'ðəʊ]	obwohl
helpless ['helpləs]	hilflos
independent [ˌɪndɪ'pendənt]	unabhängig
to **lie down** [laɪ 'daʊn]	(sich) hinlegen, niederlegen
to **lie, lay, lain** [laɪ, leɪ, leɪn]	liegen
to **feel for** ['fi:l fə]	tasten nach
no idea [ˌnəʊ‿aɪ'dɪə]	keine Ahnung
stairs (pl) [steəz]	Treppe
footstep ['fʊtstep]	Schritt
both [bəʊθ]	beide
smell [smel]	Geruch, Gestank
aftershave ['ɑ:ftəʃeɪv]	Aftershave, Rasierwasser
to **get out** [get‿'aʊt]	entkommen
to **touch** [tʌtʃ]	berühren; antippen
fuse-box ['fju:zbɒks]	Sicherungskasten
furious ['fjʊəriəs]	wütend
to **crawl** [krɔ:l]	kriechen, krabbeln; schleichen

to **grab** [græb]	greifen, schnappen
Crash! [kræʃ]	Bumm!, Krach!
to **take your chance** [ˌteɪk jɔː 'tʃɑːns]	etwas wagen, etwas riskieren
to **run upstairs** [ˌrʌn‿ʌp'steəz]	die Treppe hinaufrennen
to **lock** [lɒk]	abschließen
icon ['aɪkɒn]	Ikone
whose [huːz]	dessen, deren (Relativpronomen)
would [wʊd]	würde(n)
to **be wrong** [biː 'rɒŋ]	Unrecht haben
activity [æk'tɪvəti]	Aktivität
dark ['dɑːk]	Dunkelheit, Finsternis

1 Words for pictures

Finde die richtigen Wörter zu den Bildern.

1. ______________________________

2. ______________________________

3. ______________________________

4. ______________________________

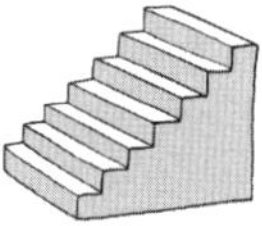

5. ______________________________

2 Weights and measurements

Schreibe auf Englisch alle Maße und Gewichtseinheiten auf, die dir einfallen.

____

____

____

3 Little words

Wie heißen die kleinen Wörter?

1. fast ________________
2. irgendwo ________________
3. dessen, deren ________________
4. bis zu ________________

4 Wordsnake

Welche Wörter sind in der Wortschlange versteckt? Finde sie und schreibe sie auf.

____

____

____

____

5 Irregular verbs

Vervollständige die Tabelle.

to take		
		stood
to lie		
	felt	
		got
	ran	
to understand		

6 Opposites

Finde das Gegenteil.

1. national ______________ 3. dirty ______________

2. moon ______________ 4. together ______________

7 Odd one out

Welches Wort fällt aus der Reihe? Markiere es.

1. cruise ocean liner stranger
2. kilometre yard meat
3. to sail lake to windsurf
4. uncle mother father
5. Irish Welsh aftershave
6. ferry port ocean liner

8 One word or two?

Setze die Wörter richtig zusammen. Achte darauf, ob sie getrennt oder zusammen geschrieben werden.

coast	ocean	any	box	where	ring
life	rubber	phone	liner	line	guard

_______________ _______________

_______________ _______________

_______________ _______________

9 German and English words

Setze die englischen Wörter ein. Unterstreiche die Unterschiede zwischen den deutschen und englischen Wörtern.

1. _______________ = Ozean
2. _______________ = sandig
3. _______________ = Kilometer
4. _______________ = Kanal
5. _______________ = Schwimmer
6. _______________ = Paradies
7. _______________ = Beginn
8. _______________ = Ikone

10 Verbs

Verbinde die Wörter richtig.

1. to take	for
2. to feel	off
3. to run	down
4. to get	lost
5. to lie	upstairs
6. to be	out

11 New words

Diese Wörter fand ich in Unit 3 besonders …

schwer zu merken	leicht zu merken	nützlich

12 Words for tomorrow

Mit welchen Wörtern hast du noch Probleme? Notiere sie und wiederhole sie morgen.

Unit 4 Let it out!

Check-in

to **let, let, let** [let, let, let]	lassen
tattoo [tæt'u:]	Tätowierung
disappointed [ˌdɪsə'pɔɪntɪd]	enttäuscht
frustrated [frʌs'treɪtɪd]	frustriert
strict [strɪkt]	streng, strikt
to **have an argument** [ˌhæv‿ən‿'ɑ:gjəmənt]	sich streiten
eyebrow ['aɪbraʊ]	Augenbraue
I want my ... pierced. [aɪ 'wɒnt maɪ ... 'pɪəst]	Ich möchte mein/e ... piercen lassen.
to **want sb to do sth** [wɒnt]	wollen, dass jemand etwas tut
direct [dɪ'rekt]	direkt
respect [rɪ'spekt]	Respekt
poetry slam ['pəʊətri ˌslæm]	Poetry Slam (Gedichtwett-bewerb)
poetry ['pəʊətri]	Lyrik
year-old [ˌjɪər‿'əʊld]	-jährig; -Jähriger/-Jährige
to **enter** ['entə]	sich beteiligen; eintreten, betreten
winner ['wɪnə]	Gewinner/Gewinnerin, Sieger/Siegerin
round [raʊnd]	Runde
to **take part in** [teɪk 'pɑ:t‿ɪn]	teilnehmen an
workshop ['wɜ:kʃɒp]	Workshop, Werkstatt
hip hop ['hɪp hɒp]	Hip-Hop
performance [pə'fɔ:məns]	Aufführung, Vorstellung
to **take place** [teɪk 'pleɪs]	stattfinden
poet ['pəʊɪt]	Dichter/Dichterin, Poet/Poetin
to **invent** [ɪn'vent]	erfinden
live [laɪv]	live
teenage ['ti:neɪdʒ]	jugendlich
poem ['pəʊɪm]	Gedicht

wish [wɪʃ]	Wunsch
for example [fər‿ɪg'zɑːmpl]	zum Beispiel
boyfriend ['bɔɪfrend]	Freund (in einer Paarbeziehung)
special ['speʃl]	besonders, speziell
to **perform** [pə'fɔːm]	aufführen, auftreten
in all [ɪn‿'ɔːl]	insgesamt, im Ganzen
organizer ['ɔːgənaɪzə]	Organisator/Organisatorin, Veranstalter/Veranstalterin
audience ['ɔːdiəns]	Publikum
slamster ['slæmstə]	Teilnehmer/Teilnehmerin an einem Poetry Slam
up to ['ʌp tə]	bis zu
each [iːtʃ]	je, jeweils
content ['kɒntent]	Inhalt
response [rɪ'spɒns]	Reaktion, Antwort

Language

disaster [dɪ'zɑːstə]	Desaster, Katastrophe
village ['vɪlɪdʒ]	Dorf
cottage ['kɒtɪdʒ]	kleines Landhaus, Ferienhaus
not even [nɒt‿'iːvn]	nicht einmal
to **hang out, hung out, hung out** [hæŋ‿'aʊt, hʌŋ‿'aʊt, hʌŋ‿'aʊt]	sich herumtreiben
steel band [ˌstiːl 'bænd]	Steelband (Band, deren Instrumente aus leeren Ölfässern bestehen)
feeling ['fiːlɪŋ]	Gefühl
useless ['juːsləs]	nutzlos
to **text** [tekst]	Textnachricht (SMS) schicken, simsen
to **put out** [pʊt‿'aʊt]	hinausstellen

Everyday English

comprehensive school [kɒmprɪˈhensɪv ˌsku:l]	Gesamtschule
to **be afraid (of)** [bi:‿əˈfreɪd]	Angst haben (vor), sich fürchten (vor)
staff [stɑ:f]	Personal; Kollegium
Lost and Found [ˈlɒst ˌənd ˈfaʊnd]	Fundbüro
Would you mind ...? [ˌwʊd jə ˈmaɪnd]	Hätten Sie/Hättest du etwas dagegen ...?
trainers [ˈtreɪnəz]	Turnschuhe
difference [ˈdɪfrns]	Unterschied
to **be welcome to do sth** [bi: ˈwelkəm]	gerne etwas tun können
library [ˈlaɪbri]	Bibliothek, Bücherei
to **miss** [mɪs]	verfehlen
secretary [ˈsekrətri]	Sekretär/Sekretärin
to **imagine** [ɪˈmædʒɪn]	sich (etwas) vorstellen
a.m. [ˌeɪˈem]	vormittags (Uhrzeit)
to **guess** [ges]	raten, vermuten
yukky [ˈjʌki]	ekelhaft
session [ˈseʃn]	Veranstaltung
shy [ʃaɪ]	schüchtern
notice board [ˈnəʊtɪs bɔ:d]	schwarzes Brett
notice [ˈnəʊtɪs]	Anschlag, Notiz
system [ˈsɪstəm]	System
abroad [əˈbrɔ:d]	im/ins Ausland
Welcome to ... [ˈwelkəm tə]	Willkommen in ...
to **compare** [kəmˈpeə]	vergleichen
compulsory [kəmˈpʌlsri]	obligatorisch, zwingend
state [steɪt]	Staat, Land; staatlich
as well as [əz ˈwel‿əz]	sowohl ... als auch
private [ˈpraɪvɪt]	privat
following [ˈfɒləʊɪŋ]	folgend/folgender/folgende/folgendes
grid [grɪd]	Gitter, Tabelle
primary school [ˈpraɪməri ˌsku:l]	Grundschule

grammar school ['græmə ˌsku:l]	Gymnasium
exam [ɪg'zæm]	Examen, Prüfung
GCSE [ˌdʒi:si:es'i:]	Prüfung zum Abschluss der Sekundarstufe
A-levels (pl) ['eɪlevlz]	brit. Abitur
possible ['pɒsəbl]	möglich
college ['kɒlɪdʒ]	College; Institut
advanced [əd'vɑ:nst]	fortgeschritten
level ['levl]	Ebene, Niveau

Get fit!

news (sg.) [nju:z]	Nachricht(en), Neuigkeit(en)
glad [glæd]	froh
to **put in** [pʊt͜'ɪn]	einschieben
extra ['ekstrə]	zusätzlich; Zusatz
training ['treɪnɪŋ]	Training, Ausbildung
lots of love [ˌlɒts͜əv 'lʌv]	viele Grüße (am Briefende)
Ha! [hɑ:]	Ha!
I wish I had ... [wɪʃ]	Ich wünschte, ich hätte ...
to **wish** [wɪʃ]	wünschen
proud of ['praʊd͜əv]	stolz auf
to **make it** ['meɪk͜ɪt]	es schaffen
to **jump about** [ˌdʒʌmp͜ə'baʊt]	herumspringen
winning goal ['wɪnɪŋ gəʊl]	Siegtreffer

Overheard

to **fight, fought, fought** [faɪt, fɔ:t, fɔ:t]	streiten, kämpfen
to **advise** [əd'vaɪz]	raten
to **stay out** [steɪ͜'aʊt]	wegbleiben
answerphone ['ɑ:nsəfəʊn]	Anrufbeantworter
speaking ['spi:kɪŋ]	am Apparat
Shall we ... ? ['ʃæl͜wi:]	Wollen wir ...?
to **be called** [bi: 'kɔ:ld]	heißen, genannt werden

Facts and fiction

mate [meɪt]	Kamerad/Kameradin, Kumpel
harm [hɑ:m]	Schaden, Verletzung
to **add** [æd]	hinzufügen, addieren
dear [dɪə]	Schatz (Anrede)
to **have a fit** [ˌhæv‿ə 'fit]	einen Anfall bekommen, Zustände kriegen
to **care** [keə]	sich kümmern, sich interessieren, wichtig nehmen
to **get into such a state** [get‿ɪntə sʌtʃ‿ə 'steɪt]	durchdrehen, (sich) verrückt machen
to **the brink** [tə ðə 'brɪŋk]	bis zur Oberkante, an den Rand
to **swerve** [swɜ:v]	ausweichen, ausscheren
curve [kɜ:v]	Kurve
alive [ə'laɪv]	lebendig
to **shake, shook, shaken** [ʃeɪk, ʃʊk, 'ʃeɪkn]	schütteln, zittern
leaf, leaves (pl) [li:f; li:vz]	Blatt
wave [weɪv]	Welle
to **go weak** [gəʊ 'wi:k]	schwach werden
weak [wi:k]	schwach
to **choke** [tʃəʊk]	ersticken, keine Luft bekommen
glee [gli:]	Entzücken

Words in action

puzzle ['pʌzl]	Rätsel, Puzzle
dictionary ['dɪkʃnri]	Wörterbuch
dance [dɑ:nts]	Tanz

1 Poetry Slam

Ergänze die fehlenden Buchstaben.

1. y__a__-__ld
2. w__nn__r
3. __nv__nt
4. t__en__ge
5. p__et__y

6 w__rk__h__p

7. sl__m__ter
8. p__rf__rm

2 Irregular verbs

Ergänze die Tabelle.

to let		
	hung out	
	got off	
to put out		
		fought
	shook	
to go		

3 Adjectives

In dieser Unit hast du viele neue Adjektive gelernt. Schreibe alle auf, die dir einfallen.

4 Small words

Wo kommen die kleinen Wörter hin?

off place out out about out

1. to take ________________
2. to hang ________________
3. to get ________________
4. to jump ________________
5. to put ________________
6. to stay ________________

5 Odd one out

Welches Wort fällt aus der Reihe?

1. A-levels	GCSE	staff	exam
2. girlfriend	love	boyfriend	session
3. poet	poetry	wish	poem
4. tattoo	pierced	eyebrow	village
5. library	cafeteria	private	classroom

6 What can you say?

Wie sagst du das auf Englisch?

1. Hätten Sie etwas dagegen…?

____

2. Du willst einen Brief mit “Viele Grüße” beenden.

____

3. Du meldest dich am Telefon mit deinem Namen.

____

7 Words for pictures

Finde die richtigen Wörter zu den Bildern.

1. ______________________

2. ______________________

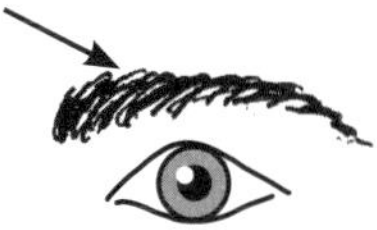

3. ______________________

4. ______________________

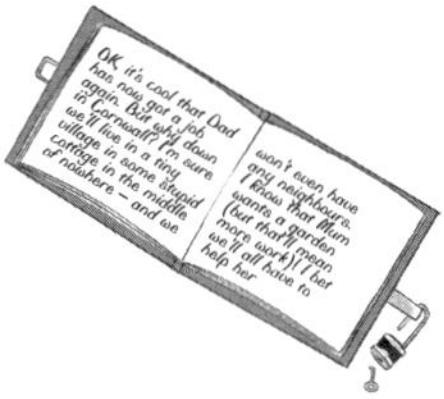

8 English or German?

Welche englischen Wörter aus Unit 4 werden ähnlich geschrieben wie im Deutschen? Schreibe fünf auf und unterstreiche die Unterschiede.

German	English

9 Wordsnake

Welche Wörter sind in der Wortschlange versteckt?

10 Poetry slam

Was gehört alles zu einem Poetry Slam?

11 New words

Diese Wörter fand ich in Unit 4 besonders …

schwer zu merken	leicht zu merken	nützlich

Unit 5 Screen shots

Check-in

screen shot ['skri:n ˌʃɒt]	Screenshot
screen [skri:n]	Bildschirm, Leinwand
shot [ʃɒt]	Schuss, Schlag
programme ['prəʊgræm]	Programm, Sendung (TV, Radio)
tough [tʌf]	hart, rau, zäh
fair [feə]	blond, hell
heroine ['herəʊɪn]	Heldin
average ['ævrɪdʒ]	durchschnittlich
daily ['deɪli]	täglich
talk show ['tɔ:k ˌʃəʊ]	Talkshow
reality show [ri'æləti ˌʃəʊ]	Realityshow
viewer ['vju:ə]	Zuschauer/Zuschauerin
industry ['ɪndəstri]	Industrie
twice [twaɪs]	zweimal
dramatic [drə'mætɪk]	dramatisch
musical ['mju:zɪkl]	Musical
seldom ['seldəm]	selten
to **kiss** [kɪs]	küssen
cartoon [kɑ:'tu:n]	Cartoon, Zeichentrickfilm
comedy ['kɒmədi]	Komödie
detective story [dɪ'tektɪv ˌstɔ:rɪ]	Krimi
documentary [ˌdɒkjə'mentri]	Dokumentarfilm
docu soap ['dɒkju ˌsəʊp]	Dokusoap
science fiction [ˌsaɪəns 'fɪkʃn]	Sciencefiction
thriller ['θrɪlə]	Thriller
myth [mɪθ]	Mythos
grave [greɪv]	Grab
script [skrɪpt]	Drehbuch

Language

pet [pet]	Haustier, Liebling
final ['faɪnl]	letzte/letzter/letztes

seaside ['si:saɪd]	Küste, Meeresküste
rescue ['reskju:]	Rettung
cook [kʊk]	Koch/Köchin
link [lɪŋk]	Verbindung, Bindeglied
host [həʊst]	Gastgeber; Talkmaster
charts (pl) [tʃɑ:ts]	Charts, Hitparade
hit [hɪt]	Hit
series, series (pl) ['sɪəri:z]	Serie
hound [haʊnd]	Jagdhund
sitcom ['sɪtkɒm]	Situationskomödie
alien ['eɪliən]	Fremder/Fremde, Außerirdischer/Außerirdische
diamond ['daɪəmənd]	Diamant
jewellery ['dʒu:əlri]	Schmuck
star [stɑ:]	Star, Stern
countdown ['kaʊntdaʊn]	Countdown
emergency [ɪ'mɜ:dʒnsi]	Notfall, Notlage
patient ['peɪʃnt]	Patient/Patientin
travel ['trævl]	Reise
on the job [ˌɒn ðə 'dʒɒb]	bei der Arbeit
runaway ['rʌnəˌweɪ]	Ausreißer/Ausreißerin
anybody ['eniˌbɒdi]	irgendjemand, jeder (beliebige)
somebody ['sʌmbədi]	jemand
He had something on his mind. [maɪnd]	Ihn beschäftigte etwas.
mind [maɪnd]	Geist, Verstand

Everyday English

guest [gest]	Gast
reception [rɪ'sepʃn]	Rezeption, Empfang
sir [sɜ:]	mein Herr (Anrede)
to **smoke** [sməʊk]	rauchen
pipe [paɪp]	Pfeife
It's no bother. ['bɒðə]	Kein Problem.
to **have a look** [ˌhæv‿ə 'lʊk]	(an)schauen, nachschauen

certainly ['sɜ:tnli]	sicher, gewiss
awful ['ɔ:fl]	schrecklich, furchtbar
to **book** [bʊk]	buchen, reservieren
Oh dear! [əʊ 'dɪə]	Oje!
review [rɪ'vju:]	Kritik

Get fit!

brave [breɪv]	tapfer, mutig
wife, wives (pl) [waɪf; waɪvz]	Ehefrau
hunting ['hʌntɪŋ]	Jagen
son [sʌn]	Sohn
to **get on** [get‿'ɒn]	aufsteigen
to **open** ['əʊpn]	sich öffnen, aufgehen
to **turn** [tɜ:n]	drehen, sich umdrehen
strong [strɒŋ]	stark
wolf, wolves (pl) [wʊlf; wʊlvz]	Wolf
tooth, teeth (pl) [tu:θ; ti:θ]	Zahn
to **attack** [ə'tæk]	angreifen
blood [blʌd]	Blut
cry [kraɪ]	Schrei
hurt [hɜ:t]	verletzt
dead [ded]	tot
shocked [ʃɒkt]	geschockt, schockiert
to **understand** [ˌʌndə'stænd]	verstehen
to **bury** ['beri]	begraben, beerdigen
gravestone ['greɪvstəʊn]	Grabstein

Overheard

crew [kru:]	Crew, Besatzung, Mannschaft
to **walk up to** [wɔ:k‿'ʌp tə]	hingehen, zugehen auf
assistant [ə'sɪstnt]	Assistent/Assistentin
director [dɪ'rektə]	Direktor/Direktorin, Regisseur/Regisseurin
couch potato ['kaʊtʃ pəˌteɪtəʊ]	Fernsehglotzer/Fernsehglotzerin, Couchpotato

Facts and fiction

to **glow** [gləʊ]	leuchten
only ['əʊnli]	einzige/einziger/einziges
inheritor [ɪn'herɪtə]	Erbe/Erbin
nephew ['nefju:]	Neffe
What's the matter? [ˌwɒts ðə 'mætə]	Was ist los?
to **solve** [sɒlv]	lösen, aufklären
mystery ['mɪstəri]	Geheimnis, Rätsel
boot [bu:t]	Stiefel
beard [bɪəd]	Bart
servant ['sɜ:vnt]	Diener/Dienerin
poor [pɔ:; pʊə]	arm
to **go for a walk** [ˌgəʊ fər‿ə 'wɔ:k]	spazieren gehen
walk [wɔ:k]	Spaziergang
to **sound** [saʊnd]	klingen, sich anhören
wild [waɪld]	wild
grey [greɪ]	grau
scientist ['saɪəntɪst]	Wissenschaftler/Wissenschaftlerin
to **die** [daɪ]	sterben
powder ['paʊdə]	Puder, Pulver
to **knock** [nɒk]	klopfen; stoßen, schlagen
bark [bɑ:k]	Bellen
to **share** [ʃeə]	teilen
myself [maɪ'self]	(ich) selbst; mich (selbst)
to **sniff** [snɪf]	schnüffeln, schnuppern
body ['bɒdi]	Körper
towards [tə'wɔ:dz]	in Richtung, auf … zu, darauf zu
gunshot ['gʌnʃɒt]	Schuss
to **echo** ['ekəʊ]	widerhallen
gun [gʌn]	Schusswaffe
to **arrest** [ə'rest]	festnehmen, verhaften

1 Words for pictures

Finde die richtigen Wörter zu den Bildern.

1. ______________________________

2. ______________________________

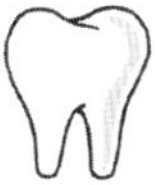

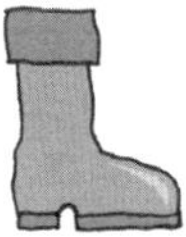

3. ______________________________

4. ______________________________

5. ______________________________

2 Little words

Wie heißen die kleinen Wörter?

1. pro ______________________________
2. selten ______________________________
3. zweimal ______________________________

3 Odd one out

Welches Wort fällt aus der Reihe?

1.	comedy	science fiction	thriller	heroine
2.	director	hound	assistant	viewer
3.	to sniff	to bark	dog	cat
4.	dead	gravestone	to glow	to bury
5.	nephew	son	wife	servant

4 Mixed words

Welche Verben verstecken sich in diesem Buchstabensalat?

1. tatakc → ____________________

2. ekoms → ____________________

3. unrt → ____________________

4. kckno → ____________________

5. wglo → ____________________

6. ffsin → ____________________

5 Who or what is it?

Welche Wörter werden hier gesucht?

1. Who tries to solve crimes? ____________________

2. Who lies in hospital? ____________________

3. Someone who you invite to your house.

   ____

6 Word puzzle

Finde die 13 Wörter im Puzzle. Sie sind senkrecht, waagerecht und diagonal versteckt.

brave, comedy, director, documentary, dramatic, guard, hero, heroine, musical, pipe, son, viewer, wife

D	N	H	E	R	O	I	N	E
O	C	P	F	N	D	V	N	D
C	J	O	J	P	I	P	E	U
U	D	H	M	E	I	S	A	H
M	H	T	W	E	G	S	G	F
E	K	E	R	U	D	T	H	E
N	R	W	A	E	R	Y	J	H
T	W	R	K	B	E	G	S	E
A	D	I	R	E	C	T	O	R
R	R	A	F	I	Z	U	N	O
Y	V	W	E	E	Z	T	Z	K
E	D	R	A	M	A	T	I	C
L	K	W	J	P	W	H	Z	G
J	M	U	S	I	C	A	L	T

7 Opposites

Finde das Gegenteil.

1. alive ____________________
2. daughter ____________________
3. to close ____________________
4. upstairs ____________________

8 Who am I?

Finde die richtigen Buchstaben.

1. The first letter of 'suspect'. ____
2. The second letter of 'script'. ____
3. The second and fifth letter of 'fiction'. ____
4. The fourth and fifth letter of 'screen'. ____
5. The last letter of 'reception'. ____
6. The second and third letter of 'attack'. ____
7. The third letter of 'alien'. ____
8. The last letter of 'towards'. ____
9. The last letter of 'arrest'. ____
10. I do a lot of experiments. ______________________

9 TV words

Was gehört alles zum Thema „Fernsehen"?

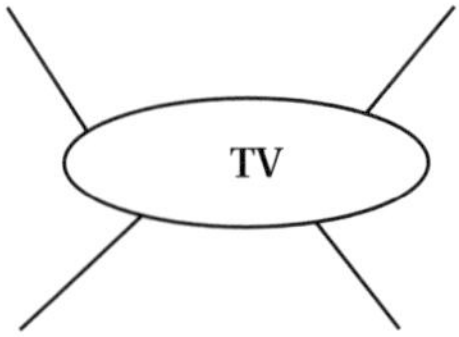

10 What's the word?

Wie heißen diese Wörter auf Englisch?

1. [bɑ:k] ________________
2. [ˈmɪstəri] ________________
3. [ˈekəʊ] ________________
4. [haʊnd] ________________
5. [kʊk] ________________
6. [ʃɒkt] ________________

11 Difficult words

Welche Wörter sind dir in dieser Unit besonder schwer gefallen? Schreibe sie auf und wiederhole sie nochmals.

____

____

____

Lösungen

Unit 1

1 1. rugby 2. player 3. baseball 4. stadium 5. pitch
6. goalkeeper 7. back line 8. referee

2 1. American football 2. rugby boot 3. back line 4. fact box
5. home plate 6. goal post

3 1. cup 2. doorstep 3. referee 4. inch 5. stand 6. birth

4 Vorschlag: pitch, helmet, glove, bat, ball, home plate, pitcher, batter, catcher, player

5 1. about 2. you/they 3. against 4. nearly 5. enough
6. across

6 1. at the bottom 2. full 3. old

7 1. catcher 2. batter 3. singer 4. player 5. teacher
6. reporter

8 1. foot 2. cup 3. helmet 4. glove

9 1. cups 2. centuries 3. pitches 4. feet 5. referees
6. goalkeepers

10 Vorschlag: to catch, to bat, to score, to kill, to send off

11 [əʊ]: row, post, lonely, home, stone
[ɒ]: across, knock
[ɔ:]: score, born
[ʌ]: glove

12 Schülerlösung

Unit 2

1 1. spectacular 2. trendy 3. rich 4. expensive 5. scary

2

R	F	D	J	J	S	N	O	N	R
M	O	A	R	E	W	E	C	T	E
F	R	Y	K	W	F	W	O	P	G
C	L	F	A	E	B	S	U	R	U
T	A	X	I	L	U	P	R	I	L
H	S	I	N	C	E	A	I	N	A
B	U	S	Y	L	U	P	E	C	R
I	A	G	A	F	T	E	R	E	K
F	S	K	E	E	T	R	F	G	N
A	D	C	H	F	J	E	N	T	D
S	D	L	C	Q	U	E	U	E	H
F	I	N	A	L	L	Y	E	R	L

3 Vorschlag: museum, palace, department store, castle, tower, house, church, school, hospital
4 1. underground 2. teenager 3. tin 4. pier 5. kind
5 1. to go far 2. to come true 3. to put out 4. to get interested
6 1. building 2. deliver 3. pollution 4. milkman 5. tradition 6. jewel 7. burn 8. company
7 1. inside 2. after 3. quarter 4. finally 5. since
8 1. scariest 2. best 3. faster 4. trendiest 5. oldest
9 1. spectacular 2. bigger 3. the scariest 4. the trendiest 5. more valuable 6. busy
10 1. view 2. relive 3. underground 4. pickpocket
11 punk
12 Schülerlösung

Unit 3

1 1. sun 2. rubber ring 3. ring 4. stamp 5. stairs
2 Vorschlag: mile, inch, yard, kilometre, pound, stone, gramme
3 1. almost 2. somewhere 3. whose 4. up to
4 travel, kilometre, passport, trolley, international, passenger, fly, European, announcement, officer, channel, ferry, land, port
5 to take – took – taken, to stand – stood – stood, to lie – lay – lain, to feel – felt – felt, to get – got – got, to run – ran – run, to understand – understood – understood
6 1. international 2. sun 3. clean 4. alone
7 1. stranger 2. meat 3. lake 4. uncle 5. aftershave 6. port
8 lifeguard, ocean liner, coastline, anywhere, phone box, rubber ring
9 1. ocean – Ozean
2. sandy – sandig
3. kilometre – Kilometer
4. channel – Kanal
5. swimmer – Schwimmer
6. paradise – Paradies

7. beginning – Beginn
8. icon – Ikone
10 1. to take off 2. to feel for 3. to run upstairs
4. to get out 5. to lie down 6. to be lost
11 Schülerlösung
12 Schülerlösung

Unit 4

1 1. year-old 2. winner 3. invent 4. teenage 5. poetry
6. workshop 7. slamster 8. perform
2 to let – let – let, to hang out – hung out – hung out,
to get off – got off – got off, to put out – put out – put out,
to fight – fought – fought, to shake – shook – shaken,
to go – went – gone
3 Vorschlag: disappointed, frustrated, strict, direct, useless,
shy, compulsory, private, glad, proud, alive, weak
4 1. to take place 2. to hang out 3. to get off
4. to jump about 5. to put out 6. to stay out
5 1. staff 2. session 3. wish 4. village 5. private
6 1. Would you mind ... ? 2. lots of love
3. Hello, it's ... speaking.
7 1. wave 2. leaf 3. eyebrow 4. diary
8 Vorschlag: Gewinner – winner, direkt – direct,
speziell – special, Desaster – disaster, Notiz – notice
9 disaster, useless, argument, content, response, village,
nowhere, feeling
10 Vorschlag: poetry, poem, judge, slamster, slam rule,
winner, round, take part, enter, workshop, performance,
poet, perform, audience
11 Schülerlösung

Unit 5

1 1. cook 2. tooth 3. boot 4. wolf 5. beard

2 1. per 2. seldom 3. twice

3 1. heroine 2. hound 3. cat 4. to glow 5. servant

4 1. attack 2. smoke 3. turn 4. knock 5. glow 6. sniff

5 1. detective 2. patient 3. guest

6

D	N	H	E	R	O	I	N	E
O	C	P	F	N	D	V	N	D
C	J	O	J	P	I	P	E	U
U	D	H	M	E	I	S	A	H
M	H	T	W	E	G	S	G	F
E	K	E	R	U	D	T	H	E
N	R	W	A	E	R	Y	J	H
T	W	R	K	B	E	G	S	E
A	D	I	R	E	C	T	O	R
R	R	A	F	I	Z	U	N	O
Y	V	W	E	E	Z	T	Z	K
E	D	R	A	M	A	T	I	C
L	K	W	J	P	W	H	Z	G
J	M	U	S	I	C	A	L	T

7 1. dead 2. son 3. to open 4. downstairs

8 scientist

9 Vorschlag: screen, programme, talk show, reality show, viewer, musical, cartoon, comedy, detective story, documentary, docu soap, science fiction, thriller, series, sitcom, star, scene

10 1. bark 2. mystery 3. echo 4. hound 5. cook 6. shocked

11 Schülerlösung

Lernen mit Filmstarbegleitung!

„Action-UK 3!" Filmsequenzen auf DVD

ISBN 978-3-12-585183-2

„Die neuen Abenteuer von Maya, Josh und Greg: Ein Filmwettbewerb führt sie in fünf Regionen Großbritanniens. Spannende Episoden im Originalton, thematisch passend zum Schülerbuch."

Wort für Wort eine echte Hilfe.

PONS Wörterbuch Orange Line

Deutsch-Engl./Engl.-Deutsch

ISBN 978-3-12-517682-9

70.000 Stichwörter und Wendungen mit dem Wortschatz der Orange Line Schülerbücher. Für alle Klassenstufen.